Minimalist Lofts

Minimalist Lofts

Publisher:
Paco Asensio

Editorial coordination and text:
Aurora Cuito

Graphic Design:
Mireia Casanovas Soley

Layout:
Emma Termes Parera / Nacho Gràcia

Translation:
Bill Bain

Copyediting:
Juliet King

2002 © First published in 2002 by LOFT and HBI, an imprint of HarperCollins Publishers
10 East 53rd St.
New York
NY 10022-5299

Distributed in the U.S. and Canada by
Watson-Guptill Publications
770 Broadway
New York
NY 10003-9595
Ph.: (800) 451-1741 or (732) 363-4511 in NJ, AK, HI Fax: (732) 363-0338

ISBN: 0-8230-3076-8

Distributed throughout the rest of the world by Harper Collins International
10 East 53rd St.
New York
NY 10022-5299
Fax: (212) 207-7654

ISBN: 0-06-008758-7

Editorial project

LOFT publications
Domènec 9, 2-2
08012 Barcelona. Spain
Tel.: +34 93 218 30 99
Fax: +34 93 237 00 60
e-mail: loft@loftpublications.com
www.loftpublications.com

Printed by:
Tesys Industria Gráfica. Barcelona, Spain

May 2002

Minimalist Lofts

Loft living is one of the main trends of urban development. This trend has already led to a migration towards urban areas, the resurgence of city centers and, above all, to the birth of a new conscience. The inhabitants of a loft protect a city's architectural past by making it, along with art, a part of daily life.

The term loft initially meant an open, diaphanous space located in an indus-

trial building or unused warehouse. Of English origin, the word also referred to an attic or the upper level of a factory. Today, however, the concept of a loft has a new meaning: a large, renovated space whose industrial architecture is used for domestic purposes. Besides defining an architectural style, the word loft also describes the resident's new lifestyle.

The presented here lofts were rehabil-

itated with precise alterations meant to equip the space for its new residents without completely modifying it. These projects were guided by minimalist strategies understood as guidelines intended to preserve individual con-structional elements. This is not a mini-malism associated only with smooth surface areas and the color white;this is a minimalism used to created practical and flexible homes that satisfy the

architect and clients' wishes with few architectural gestures.

The results are simple domestic spaces in which the structural elements serve as decoration, creating a warm space without the use of artful devices.

Lofts are open, airy spaces often located in old industrial buildings. Conversions of these spaces tend to expose the framing system and installations and to preserve the structure's original manufacturing origins. The projects collected in this book involve flexible dwellings that adapt to the functional needs of their users, and at the same time, permit a varied domestic use of their rooms.

The book includes more than twenty-five lofts refurbished with a minimalist design. The creative process has been reduced to the basic concepts of light, volume and mass. The formalization of all the projects is austere, but conceals a technical and well-developed construction that permits a clear and striking perception of the interiors.

The introduction's selection of photographs attempts to show the most representative building elements of these lofts.

Structure. In the majority of cases, the load-bearing frame is not only used to advantage, it is also emphasized and becomes a major element in the renovation. The conservation of metal columns, the elimination of false ceilings in order to recover the brick archways, or the cleaning of concrete beams are some of the methods employed.

Finishings. The architects as well as the clients exhibit very different needs, and thus a wide variety of materials come under consideration. Each individual employs different facings according to the result being elicited. But in the projects presented here, one may appreciate a common affinity for smooth, glossy, clean surfaces contrasting with rough finishings, the latter normally conserved from the pre-existing buildings. The result is a minimalist space subtly marked by traces from the past.

Divisions. The diaphanous quality of lofts is maintained by the use of ethereal partitioning that is not all that obviously present in the spaces. Some designers have opted for sliding doors that disappear behind walls, others for mobile screens that permit alterations in the space distribution, and almost all have put to good use translucent materials to aid light flow through the separate spaces.

Windows. Industrial buildings often boast large windows that allow efficient ventilation and supply abundant natural light. Thus, the majority of clients prefer not to replace these features. At times, it is necessary to replace the original woodwork with aluminum to assure watertightness, which, of course, alters the original look of the windows.

Installations. The habitability of lofts depends in large measure on their installations. The roominess of the premises makes it necessary to install good lighting and an efficient air-conditioning system to guarantee the comfort of those who live there. In the majority of the dwellings, electrical installations and ventilation tubes have been left exposed to avoid apertures in the walls. Access to the system is thus assured in case of making repair or maintenance work, and the original industrial aspect of the interiors is also conserved.

Recycling. Reuse of part of the pre-existing building is a constant in these refurbishing projects. Almost all of them put some materials and elements to their original use or give them a new use. This provision is a very coherent action in maintaining the loft's original air and, of course, it also means considerable cost reduction.

Metal beams and columns

Concrete structure

Exposed concrete columns

Cross structure of metal rail lighting

Plaster, glass and parquet

Concrete, stainless steel and wood

Wood, concrete and resin

Wood, concrete and plaster

A wood and glass divider

Translucent separation

Wire mesh sliding door

Glass partitions

Windows in the upper portion of the façade

Sloping skylight

Light softened by metal Venetian blinds

Glass façade of the interior courtyard

Exposed tubed wiring and airconditioning ducts

Airconditioning ducts

An unpartitioned bath

The kitchen dining room opens up into the living room

recycling

Metal flooring used for the partition wall

Hospital cabinets used as wardrobes

Cleaned brick

Reused refrigerator doors

Loft in London

The firm Child Graddon Lewis converted this quintessential Victorian building in the heart of Covent Garden into loftstyle apartments. They created twenty-two shell dwellings in the 32,000 square-foot building, which was originally designed as a warehouse and later used as reading rooms for the British Library. The apartments are distributed on six floors with retail space on the ground floor.

Internally, flexibility lies at the heart of the design concept, with each unit capable of linking laterally or vertically with others to create apartments ranging in size from 1,000 to over 4,000 square feet. On the market as shell apartments, the architects' adaptable design gives clients the freedom to create their own interior plan and develop their own truly unique space in this muchsoughtafter quarter of London.

The firm also designed the kitchen, the bathroom and some of the furniture, which can be purchased when buying one of the properties.

Externally, the designers refurbished the historic building to create a stunning rear elevation which capitalizes on period details. Sensitive additions include large sliding doors leading to balconies and terraces constructed with cedar decking, new metal-framed windows and panels of glass blocks that take advantage of the natural light each apartment receives. The new sloping roof at the penthouse level was clad in slate to match the original.

Turning to the other side of the building, the front elevation was remodeled to accommodate glass shopfronts flanking the building's reception area. The entrance features stone flooring and lighting that enhances the materials and the atmosphere.

Child Graddon Lewis

Architects: Child Graddon Lewis   **Collaborators:** Sandy Brown Associates (structures)   **Photographer:** Dennis Gilbert / View   **Location:** London, UK
Completion date: 2000   **Floor space:** 1,000-4,000 sq. ft.

Floor plan

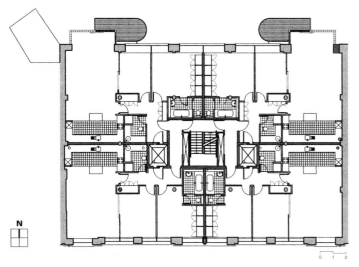

Detail of one of the partitions made of curved plastic tubes that divides the huge living room. The distance between the partitions makes it easy to recognize objects on the other side, but they separate different areas visually.

The beautiful kitchen in the show flat was designed by the architects and is an optional feature of the dwelling.

The sink and floors are made of wood and the walls are faced in stone. The kitchen is a very practical and comfortable part of the house.

N

0 1 2

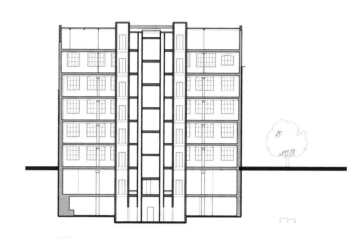

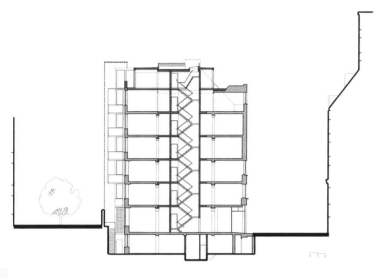

Section

Section

A wood partition separates the bedroom from the living room and houses the electrical installations. It does not include a door and thus enhances spatial flow.

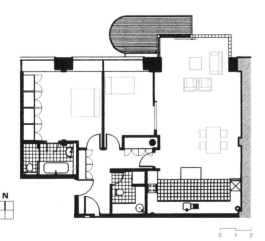

N

0 1 2

Greenberg Loft

The Smith-Miller & Hawkinson team was charged with refurbishing this loft to accommodate a dwelling and an art exhibition area. Since the client, a collector, wanted these two functions to coexist without strict borders, the architects developed a design that merges the gallery with the private spaces.

The duplex space includes a lower floor with the master bedroom, the living room, the dining room, the kitchen, the projection room, a painting studio, a storeroom and a large terrace. The upper floor contains two sub-levels, guest rooms and a studio. These work areas did not exist in the original configuration, but the designers took advantage of the height of the ceilings to install them, using reinforced concrete on black-painted steel rails and temperedglass guard rails. The same concrete was also used on the upper floor in some columns and facings. In general, however, the architects chose white plaster for the dividers and a birchwood floor.

One of the project's most interesting features is the division of the space by partitions joined to the floor's lowered baseboard, creating the sensation of weightlessness. These elements, together with enormous sliding wood-veneer doors, create flexible, interconnecting spaces.

The architects also reformed the north façade, which is slightly inclined, by installing large, motorized windows that fill the living/dining room with light and offer splendid views of the city. To complement the lighting, spotlights were suspended from the rails that support the doors and false ceiling.

Smith-Miller & Hawkinson Architects

Architects: Smith-Miller&Hawkinson Architects   Photographer: Matteo Piazza   Location: New York, New York, US   Completion date: 1997   Floor space: 6,000 sq. ft.

Mixed materials are the project's main feature. Just as the building's frame includes the coexistence of industrial and conventional solutions, the furnishings also combine contemporary design with eighteenth and nineteenth century sculpture.

Construction detail of the door

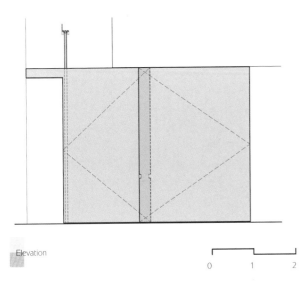

Elevation

0   1   2

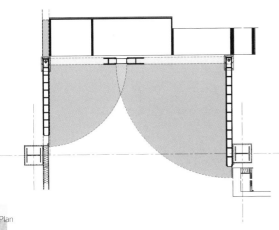

Plan

The sliding doors can close off
the spaces in different ways.
The images on this page
show how these doors
define the studio.

1. Entrance
2. Living room
3. Dining room
4. Kitchen
5. Master bedroom
6. Bath
7. Projection room
8. Closet
9. Painting studio
10. Recreation room
11. Guest room
12. Second sub-level
13. Studio

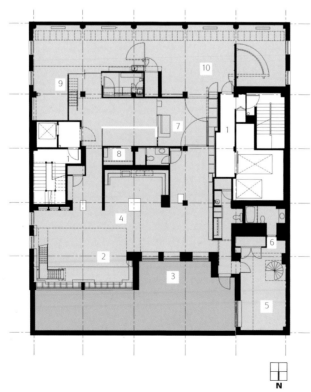

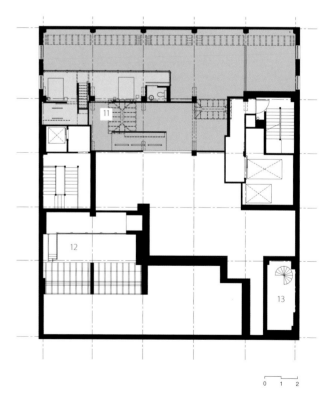

N

0 1 2

The living room and the salon are markedly expansive, airy spaces. The sub-level is joined to these spaces and is protected by a glass handrail. The natural light that filters in through the skylight and the motorized windows in the façade is complemented by spotlights in the ceiling.

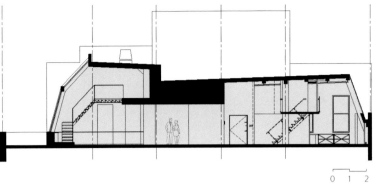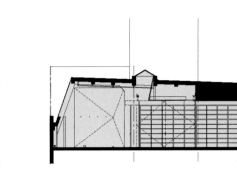

Sections

In addition to artwork, the loft owner's other major interest is multimedia machines, for which a special room has been reserved on the lower floor. A computer controls the video and audio apparatus as well as an enormous viewing screen, concealed in the false ceiling.

Residence in Toronto

This residence is located in an old industrial neighborhood on Toronto's east side. Recently, photographers, artists and other professionals have moved into this revitalized zone, and this particular project is one of many. The reforms in the area's warehouses and factories are being carried out along with urban planning and the introduction of businesses and urban furnishings.

The aim of the designers was to create a space in which the original structure and the new elements would complement each other. The loft was originally divided into two sections that merged into a single cohesive space. The old truss system was preserved and the floors and columns were newly installed to retain the original color and texture and to create a rustic effect.

The house was constructed using some storage cabinets found in an old factory, some enormous refrigerator doors and some recycled pieces from a cafeteria as base units. To match these, Cecconi and Simone designed a kitchen counter, a bed with incorporated lighting and a piece of furniture for the office.

The windows were left untouched because their large dimensions offered extraordinary ventilation and outstanding views of the city of Toronto.

The domestic space was conceived for total flexibility: the curtains, hung from rods in the ceiling, can be moved to change the domicile's configuration. They can also be arranged to create a single room. This concept is apparent in other furnishings in the dwelling, such as the bed on wheels which can be moved around.

These strategies have created a unique architecture to which the occupants can add their own style.

Cecconi Simone Inc.

Architect: Cecconi Simone Inc. Photographer: Joy Von Tiedemann Location: Toronto, Canada Completion date: 1999 Floor space: 3,000 sq. ft.

1. Entrance
2. Kitchen
3. Bathroom
4. Closet
5. Living room
6. Dining room
7. Living room
8. Studio
9. Bedroom
10. Bathroom

N

0 1 2

The installations were left visible to reflect the building's industrial past. Both the tubes containing the electrical wiring and the water pipes run across the ceiling.

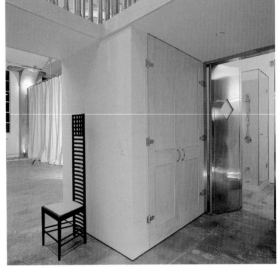

The bed, one of the pieces created by Cecconi and Simone specifically for this residence, has a mobile solid wood base with a moveable canopy that regulates the degree of privacy.

Flat and Studio in London

The motivating force behind the work of these young architects is their desire to create inspiring and productive spaces for creative activities. Their design approach, direct and unrestricted, is based on the interpretation of and reaction to the clients' needs.

The design of this London loft demonstrates Blockarchitecture's interest in redirecting the experience, the space and the materials, all of the process predicated on an unwavering commitment to new configurations within the contemporary "snip & cut" cultural context.

The idea was to keep the concrete frame, which defines and contains the entire space, as complete and open as possible. The dimensions and form of the shell are emphasized by the strong relief of the wooden floor, cut to fit the main flow of space toward the balconies on the east front of the building.

A thirty-foot wall built of recycled steel panels dominates and organizes the dwelling and defines a hall, a small storeroom, a bathroom (separate from the toilet) and a photographer's darkroom. When the doors are closed, the apartment has an isolated feel, without street access and outside communication.

The rest of the household functions, the kitchen and bath, are located beside the opposite wall. The shower and bathroom space is marked off as if it were a different room, on a concrete floor that floats above the wood floor, but without partition walls or curtains. Thanks to the distribution of the storage rooms on two sides, the apartment becomes a large area which can be used for many different activities without establishing either sleeping quarters or a "living room". It's just one big, multifunctional space.

Blockarchitecture

Architects: Blockarchitecture **Photographer:** Chris Tubbs **Location:** London, UK **Completion date:** 1998 **Floor space:** 1,900 sq. ft.

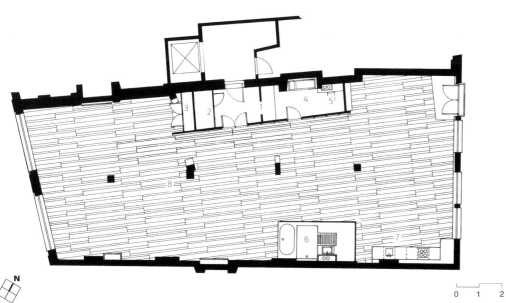

1. Entrance
2. Storeroom
3. Closet
4. Darkroom
5. Toilet
6. Bathroom
7. Kitchen
8. Multi-use space

The photos on this page show different details of the partition that marks off the storage and utility areas.

N

0　1　2

The bathtub is set on a raised concrete dais that stands out against the background of the apartment's wooden floor, giving the tub an unusual emphasis. Some of the decorative pieces are recycled.

Some of the apartment's lighting installations are focused on the ceiling to highlight the restoration work on the support beams.

Siegel Swansea Loft

Writer Joel Siegel and his wife, painter Ena Swansea, bought this New York City loft to create a space where they could both live and work. From the outset, the original character of the building, an early twentieth-century factory, was respected. The vaulted ceiling, plastered walls, and industrial details were retained. This approach was extended further by restoration work using similar products and materials and by leaving electrical installations and pipes exposed. These subtly emphasized the original features of the building, although new techniques were used to rigorously and precisely feature the details.

The studio, north-facing, allows the artist to contemplate the panoramic views through large windows, inspiring when the sun edges out from behind the clouds or hammers down on clear days. It is an open space which opens onto the living area, but there is no direct visual link because the office occupies the center of the loft, a space for relaxation and entertainment as well as work. This is a private domain; the couple unwinds here. So it is visually and acoustically isolated from the rest of the dwelling. The separation is underscored by the fact that it is the only room preserving the original wood flooring, which makes it an island surrounded by the rest of the apartment.

The most private areas, the bedrooms, bathrooms, and dressing room, are on the edges, partitioned off from the other areas.

The original floor was covered with an epoxy-urethane compound. To avoid excessive color, the vertical partitions were finished with a filler which produced a grayish, balanced, neutral ambience that creates an understated elegance.

Abelow Connors Sherman Architects

Architects: Abelow Connors Sherman Architects   **Collaborator:** Marcus Donagh   **Photographer:** Michael Moran   **Location:** New York, New York, US   **Completion date:** 1997   **Floor space:** 2,680 sq. ft.

1. Bedroom
2. Living room
3. Dining room
4. Multimedia space
5. Kitchen
6. Studio
7. Bathroom
8. Dressing room

N

0   1   2

The original floor was covered with an epoxy-urethane compound. The vertical partitions were left unpainted. Instead, a product normally used as a filler was applied. These specifically chosen materials created a grayish, neutral balance in which the works of art can be properly viewed.

The kitchen, dining room, and living room blend into the studio, which is located right next to the large windows. The magnificent views of the city are always a source of inspiration for the artist.

Loft in Tribeca

This loft sits on the western edge of Manhattan overlooking the Hudson River. It is situated next to the entrance to the Holland Tunnel, connects the island of Manhattan to New Jersey. The dwelling has a view of the cooling towers which rise above the river and vent the tunnel below. The strong industrial aesthetics of the exterior counterpoint the interior, which is deliberately drawn as clean and light. The residence was created in an old commercial space for heavy machinery. The architects installed maple wood floors in the apartment to soften the building's concrete character. French limestone provides a durable surface for the entry and defines an east-west pathway that connects the kitchen to the entrance hallway. A vertical partition made of sand-blasted glass runs north-south, separating the bedrooms from the rest of the space. A shoji screen-like sliding panel controls the loft's level of openess. The use of frosted glass provides privacy without blocking the flow of light. Whitewash over the rough-hewn concrete beams and existing masonry walls adds a touch of refinement without diminishing the original character of the space. All the cabinetry and shelving is custom designed in painted wood and clear maple.

Roughly square in plan, the loft is surrounded by windows on three sides. The dining room is located in the center and is symbolically the heart of the space. The bathrooms provide a visual oasis from the industrial views. Simple maple medicine cabinets double as framed mirrors. The glass wall and pathway intersect to define the northeastern corner, where the kitchen is located. The use of stainless steel and maple provides a functional yet warm environment in the kitchen.

Tow Studios

Architects: Peter Tow   **Photographer:** Björg Photography   **Location:** New York, US   **Completion date:** 1999   **Floor space:** 2,000 sq. ft.

Details of the living room
furniture, which is the same
pale tone as most of the
elements in the house.

View of the living room and the
sliding glazed panels that separate
the living room from the private
areas. The table is made of maple
wood, as are the floors and other
furnishings, such as the shelves
and kitchen counters.

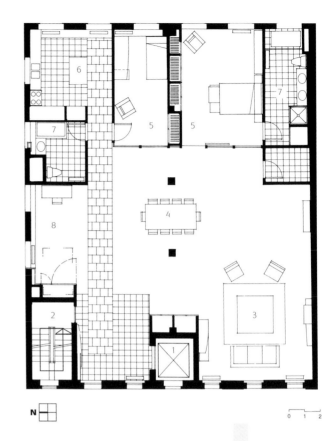

1. Elevator
2. Building staircase
3. Living room
4. Dining room
5. Bedrooms
6. Kitchen
7. Bathrooms
8. Studio

The architect left the original structure, a trabeated system, intact. It has been painted white to match the rest of the elements in the house.

Below. These images show how
the sunlight and the lighting
system illuminate the rooms.

The kitchen, in stainless steel
and maple wood, has marvelous
views of the old industrial
neighborhood of Tribeca thanks
to its enormous windows.

Actor's Residence

This project transformed a factory-warehouse into a residential building. While the architect left the 14.7-foot-high original ceilings intact in order to preserve the building's industrial character, the new dwellings have their own definite personality.

Each floor was divided into four areas of 1,606 square feet. The apartment described here, of 1,180 square feet, resulted from subdividing one of these areas into two. The division carried with it the advantage of occupying a corner of the building, thus guaranteeing an abundance of natural light. The owner's acting profession pretty well determined the desired type of space. The apartment would need, for example, room for rehearsals and performances. Space, light, and versatility became the project's main priorities.

The pre-existing structure, including the metal main beams and columns, the ceiling of ribbed arches, and even the large industrial windows, was maintained. The plan was divided in two. On one side, in a single space, the architect placed the kitchen, the dining room and the living room and on the other side, the bedroom, the bath, the toilet and the studio. The first, more public area, preserves the original high ceilings and takes advantage of in-coming light. The second area, however, adds a working level by lowering the ceiling. The lower half of this new space gives the sensation of intimacy in its more private areas. The upper half opens up a 4-foot-high space containing a library. The two levels are connected by a wooden stairway.

The walls and ceilings of the loft have been painted exclusively in white. The expected note of color comes from the library, where blue light reflects off the wooden floor in every direction.

Franc Fernández

Architect: Franc Fernández   **Photographers:** Joan Mundó, Mar Requena   **Location:** Barcelona, Spain   **Completion date:** 1997   **Floor space:** 1,180 sq. ft.

1. Entrance
2. Bedrooms
3. Bathroom
4. Living room
5. Dining room
6. Kitchen

N

0 1 2

The architect sought an austere
layout in which negative space
does not detract from the richness
of the geometric solutions.
A low budget does not have
to mean modest results.

The space containing the bedroom,
the bath, the toilet and the studio
uses water-varnished wood. The
rooms are connected by way of
sliding doors—some of translucent
glass—that reduce solid barriers.

Restoring an attic

The project entailed the restoration of an attic apartment in the historic center of Milan. The 968-square-foot space was transformed into a modern, sophisticated and elegant loft.

The architect disregarded the space's former layout and focused on a new plan. The general concept was to integrate all the rooms into a single space, thus avoiding doors and interior partitions. The choice of only one type of flooring, dark wood, also contributes to a feeling of unity. The floor's tone contrasts with the clean, white walls and inclined ceilings.

The client and the architect worked closely together throughout the entire project and opted to start from scratch. They followed abstract concepts that enabled the residence to evolve during the renovation process. The space's old functions were replaced with useful, simple and innovative forms.

Keeping in mind the sloped ceilings, the architect created a principal axis of circulation in the center of the dwelling, where the ceilings are the highest. The spaces for activities related to leisure and relaxation were constructed in the perimeter.

The service areas–the bathroom, the kitchen and the cabinets–are monolithic volumes. When reduced to simple forms, they become works of plastic arts that give new meaning to the spatial perception. Both functional and eccentric, the volumes lack instrumental validity and teeter on the edge of irony and provocation.

Since this attic apartment is a clear succession of spaces with no defined frontiers, the entrance becomes the living room, and the bedroom melts into the bathroom.

Marco Savorelli

Architects: Marco Savorelli   **Collaborator:** Luca Mercatelli   **Photographer:** Matteo Piazza   **Location:** Milan, Italy   **Completion date:** 1999   **Floor space:** 968 sq. ft.

The bathtub, a quadrilateral stone, and the shower, made of glass, are located in the bedroom. Both elements appear as independent volumes that are visually connected to the rest of the room. Only the toilet is separated by a partition wall.

Like all the rooms in the apartment, the kitchen is open and connected to the living room. The kitchen includes two cabinets, one of which contains the installations and is placed against two structural pillars that conceal the water pipes.

1. Living room
2. Kitchen
3. Toilet
4. Bathtub
5. Bedroom
6. Shower
7. Living room

N

0   1   2

The sofas were designed following
the project guidelines: floating wooden
bodies and cushions covered in a light-
colored cloth that combines with
the surroundings decorated
in the same tones.

Given the lack of vertical partitions
that mark off domestic functions, a
spare palette of materials was chosen
to unify the setting.

The attic's big sloping windows are reminiscent of the garrets of past times and let in abundant natural light. The artificial lighting comes from a spot system discreetly placed at different points in the loft.

Potter Loft

Located in New York's Chelsea district, this loft responds to the client's simple lifestyle. The floor plan is distributed according to the flow of open space that moves through the central kitchen and the nuclei comprising the baths and the bedrooms at the back of the apartment. This room is surrounded by different types of surfaces that define the thresholds of the space. Through these, different functions are distributed, and the face work is varied. Concrete panels identify the living room. Banks of lights in the dining room ceiling, including a unique overhead wedge lamp, provide intense illumination. The well-equipped kitchen space is in a centrally located area along with one of the adjacent areas of this main space.

Together, both kitchen and dining room boast twenty bars, or segments of light, connected to individual adjustable controls.

Border spaces open and close to access through the use of movable elements that slide, pivot, or roll. Constructed with a tailor-made metal panel, the sliding door is the building's security door. The pivot door, on the other hand, provides the bedroom with more privacy and allows light to pass according to its degree of openness. The windows to the street allow exterior views and maintain privacy by way of Venetian blinds that also aid the flow of light.

The entire composition of surfaces, both visual and tactile, is the result of a subtle definition of use all through the articulated series of spaces.

Resolution: 4 Architecture

Architects: Resolution: 4 Architecture **Photographer:** Eduard Hueber **Location:** New York, New York, US **Completion** date: 1999 **Floor space:** 1,075 sq. ft.

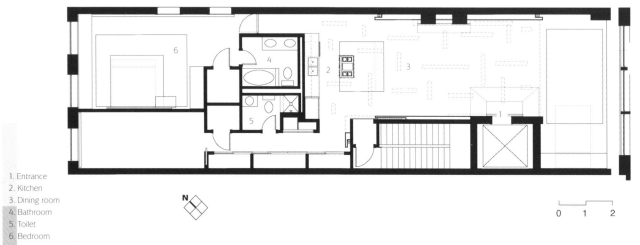

1. Entrance
2. Kitchen
3. Dining room
4. Bathroom
5. Toilet
6. Bedroom

N

0 1 2

The loft has preserved
the original face work
of one of the walls:
of cleaned brick.

The entrance door is
a sliding metal panel that
conceals access both
from the elevator and
from the stairway.

Davol Loft

The building that contains the Davol loft is one of many being renovated in the old industrial areas of New York City's lower Manhattan. This zone is slowly changing as the factories of bygone years are converted into dwellings, as new apartment buildings go up, and as public services arrive.

This project began with an empty rectangular box with the typical characteristics of a loft (columns down the center, enormous windows, a ceiling more than ten feet high) in a former industrial warehouse. The concrete columns, ceiling and floor support the beams that stretch across the building.

This distinctive spatial configuration presented a challenge if living space and a fully operational work area were to be integrated, made even more demanding by the fact that natural light had to reach the central area. The clients, two journalists, needed separate bedrooms with attached baths, a kitchen, a small storage room, a large open space for the living room and a flexible work area for each of them. The architects, once he understood clients´needs, worked artfully on a modest budget, leaving open the possibility that, in the future, better-quality finishings could be installed.

The architects placed the service areas against the windowless north and south walls. They avoided total visual separation of these rooms from the rest of the loft, treating them like modules inserted into a container. The walls of the rooms do not reach the ceiling and iridescent materials are used, creating magnificent reflective patterns that accentuate the lightness of the components.

Moneo Brock Studio

Architects: Moneo Brock Studio **Collaborators:** Alicia Velázquez, Christian Mitman **Photographer:** Michael Moran **Location:** New York, wNew York, US
Completion date: 1999 **Floor space:** 2,400 sq. ft.

Some of the partitions are moveable, making it easy to redistribute the apartment's space. The panels' translucency permits a distinctive spatial relationship and avoids permanent compartmentalization.

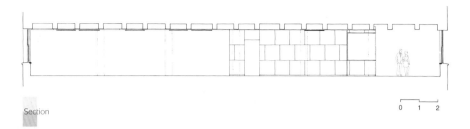

Section

0   1   2

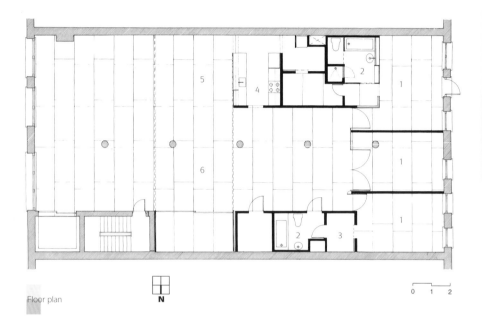

Floor plan

N

0   1   2

1. Bedrooms
2. Bathroom
3. Closet
4. Kitchen
5. Dining room
6. Multifunctional space

The finishes produce a pattern of colors, reflections, and transparencies. The extraordinary impression left by the space is the result of intense experimentation with the materials.

The translucent interior partitions allow partial observation of activities in the various rooms. The kitchen shelves can be seen from the dining room.

Floor with projecting roof

The clients' open-mindedness was important: from the beginning they accepted the risk and challenge of experimenting with new materials. Their enthusiasm provided the impetus for the creation of this opalescent oasis from which the sunset can be admired firsthand.

This large, multiuse space must meet certain acoustic requirements because the clients often use it to rehearse.

Conversion of an Old Factory

The reformation of this thirty-year-old factory and its extensive warehouse was designed to include dwellings of various sizes, offices and commercial spaces. The building was intented to be a bustling urban axis in East London on the bank of the Thames.

London's urban authority required the building's role to be that of a dynamic setting for multiple professional and recreational activities. The result reflects the complexity of the contemporary lifestyle and incorporates elements that integrate the new building into its surrounding neighborhood. For example, the building contains a bar and a gallery that promote the social character of the conversion.

The introduction of three shafts to house electrical and communications cables obviated the need for long halls and gave rise to more intimate communal areas. The structure's identity is reinforced by the application of different colors for each of the three zones.

The units destined to be used as residences are located above the ground floor. They include terraces, balconies and interior patios. While designed individually thanks to the clients' own personal involvement, the firm of Child Graddon Lewis was responsible for designing the pilot apartment that demonstrates the project's potential.

The apartments are spaces that the clients may organize as they wish. The installations were centralized, leaving the rest of the area free for rooms that do not need running water, such as the bedrooms, the living room and the studio. The electrical installations were left uncovered to facilitate the arrangement of the plugs and switches.

Child Graddon Lewis

Architects: Child Graddon Lewis   **Collaborators:** Bovis Lelliot, Rob Welling Associates   **Photographer:** Johnathan Moore   **Location:** London, UK
Completion date: 2000   **Floor space:** 535-1,075 sq. ft.

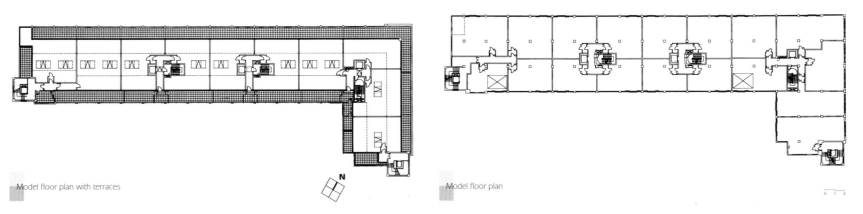

Model floor plan with terraces

N

Model floor plan

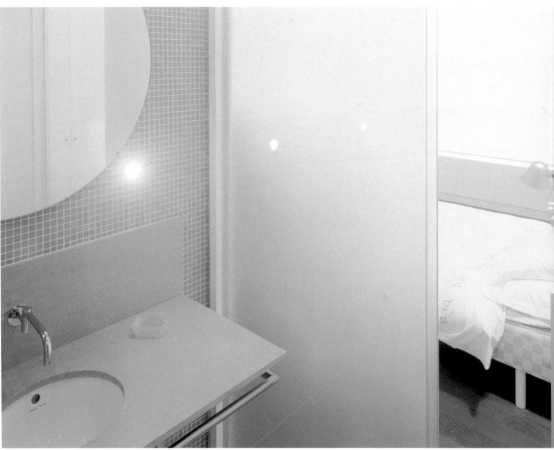

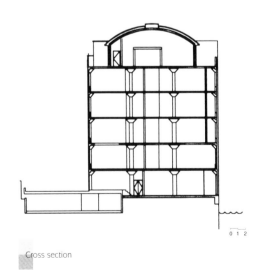

The bedrooms and the baths, while more conventional, also include sliding door systems or moveable partitions.

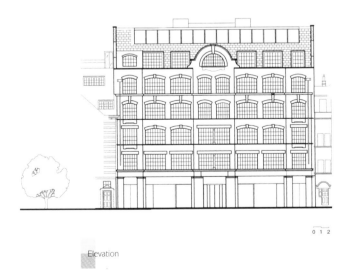

0 1 2

Elevation

0 1 2

Cross section

The model apartment has the diaphanous atmosphere common to lofts. In the living room area, moveable shelves can be used in a variety of ways as dividers.

Living and Working in a Loft

The building in Barcelona's Gracia Quarter, where this project is located, was originally a factory specializing in electrical material. The loft occupies the building's top floor, a privileged space since it enjoys private and direct access to the rooftop terrace.

The client wanted to refurbish the apartment and convert it for use as both a dwelling and office. Another prerequisite of the renovation was to keep the diaphanous, open space that had originally captivated the owner. It was equally important to assure closure of the most private rooms and the storage spaces to keep them independent of the other rooms while maintaining spatial continuity. Independent "boxes" were designed to contain the baths, the kitchen, and the cupboards. The living room, the office and the bedrooms surround the boxes. This keeps the natural light flowing into the dwelling's main spaces and allows it to filter into the floor plan's inner zones.

Large sliding doors located on the free-standing volumes permit the client to control privacy at will. At the same time, the closed areas never interfere with perception of the loft as a single, continuous, open space.

Large, intense paintings personalize each space. The artwork can be comfortably appreciated from the generous distance generated by the expansiveness of the loft.

A metal staircase leads to the upper level, where there is a small room used as an office and that leads onto the landscaped rooftop terrace.

The brick exterior walls, the original metal structure and the vaulted ceiling are original features. The dark wood flooring is new, as are the independent volumes, covered in plaster and painted white.

Helena Mateu Pomar

Architects: Helena Mateu Pomar   **Photographer:** Jordi Miralles   **Location:** Barcelona, Spain   **Completion date:** 1999   **Floor space:** 1,660 sq. ft.

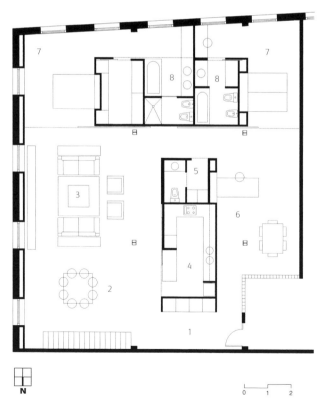

1. Entrance
2. Dining room
3. Living room
4. Kitchen
5. Toilet
6. Office
7. Bedrooms
8. Bathrooms

The one-directional texture of the ribs in the vaulted ceiling contrasts with the planes of the polished dark wood floor.

N

0   1   2

The private spaces are able
to incorporate the rest
of the space through the use
of sliding doors on metal rails.

Attic in Vienna

The renovation of this attic in Vienna is characterized by the application of energy-saving ideas usually adapted only to other architectural spaces. While the main concerns in residential architecture are functional or aesthetic, Lichtblau & Wagner were keen to eliminate any wastefulness and, in order to archieve greater efficency, these young Austrian architects ruled out all superficial luxuries like marble bathrooms, pointless terraces and grandiose entrances to concentrate on a flexible project that economizes energy, spending and space. Four basic units were conceived of 530 square feet each. They are organized in pairs and with an additional space that may be added to one apartment or the other. This alteration is easy to put into practice due to the simple relocation of partitions. The common spaces house a storeroom, a laundry and a multipurpose space for meetings or parties, which offsets the lack of space in the studios.

The bathroom outlets have been installed in the floor, like electrical plugs, in order to avoid unnecessary apertures in the partitions. The kitchen and the bath occupy a suggested position but may be moved without any alteration or reform work. The client can rearrange the dwelling according to taste or use requirements.

Another advantage of the project is the efficient use of the surface area, which takes full advantage of the space's small size. Passageways have been eliminated by placing closets and toilet facilities on the perimeter so that they do not block the interior spaces and can be used freely.

Lichtblau & Wagner

Architects: Lichtblau & Wagner   **Photographers:** Andreas Wagner, Margherita Spiluttini   **Location:** Vienna, Austria   **Completion date:** 1998   **Floor space:** 530 sq. ft.

This space beneath the sliding windows may be used as a terrace, a gallery or a greenhouse. Curtains separate this space from the rest of the dwelling, and create a sensation of warmth and comfort.

1. Bath
2. Storage
3. Kitchen
4. Entrance
5. Multiuse space
6. Installations

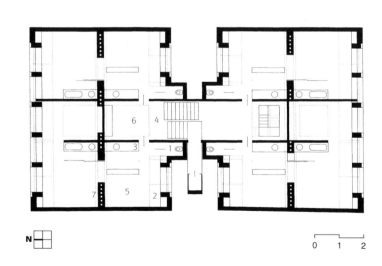

N

0   1   2

The solar panels provide eight apartments with hot water, and the centralized heating system saves both energy and space. Good thermal insulation and passive solar energy contribute to reduced heating and cooling costs.

From a construction point of view, the absence of interior walls contributes to cost reduction. Moreover, the installations are in the floor, thus obviating the need for sockets in vertical partitions. The kitchen and bathroom units are collapsible and are connected to the drains through holes in the floor.

Lichtblau & Wagner's bathrooms are linked to the living areas. They are not conceived as hermetic units, and are lit by natural light, offering daytime views of the area.

Crepain Residence

This project entailed renovating an industrial park in the center of Antwerp, Belgium. The architect converted an old, fin de siècle warehouse into a living space and office for his own use. At the same time, a thirty-year-old office complex was demolished to allow the creation of a garden and a parking lot.

The architect's workshop occupies the first two floors. The residence itself, on the third and fourth floors, combines domestic uses and the functions of a large exhibition space for an art collection.

The central design aim was to restore the original building and respect its elements. Good examples of the success of this concept are seen in the efficacy of the preservation of the barrel roofs and the reopening of some of the windows that had been boarded over. The only new volumetric mass is the core of the new elevator, which also serves as a structural center around which the rooms are arranged. The elevator also houses the main part of the vertical installations.

The dwelling's living quarters are located on the top level, arranged around the splendid west-facing terrace. The living room is thirteen feet high and enjoys panoramic views of the city, with the roofs and cathedral spires in the background. The kitchen and the bathrooms are close to the elevator shaft, where all the electrical installations are housed.

The remodeling of the Crepain residence was done entirely with concrete. This material was treated in different ways according to the architectural element that was needed. It was painted black in the elevator shaft, covered with aluminum on the terrace, and covered with dark wood where a warmer finish was needed.

Jo Crepain Architects

Architects: Jo Crepain Architects   **Collaborators:** Van Rijmenant NV   **Photographers:** Jan Verlinde, Ludo Noël   **Location:** Antwerp, Belgium   **Completion date:** 1998   **Floor space:** 13,300 sq. ft.

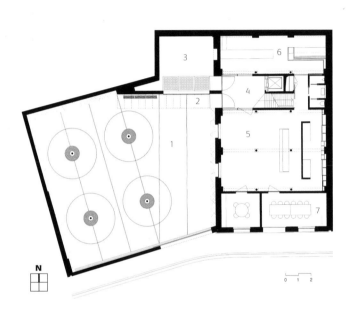

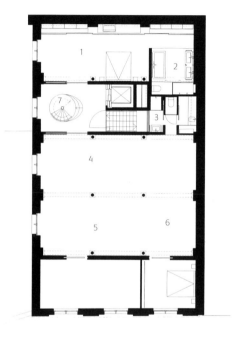

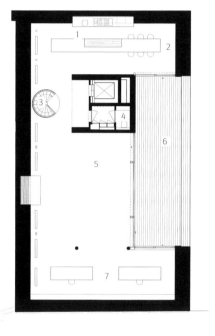

Ground floor
1. Parking lot
2. Bicycle parking
3. Garage
4. Entrance
5. Reception
6. Jo Crepain's office
7. Conference room

Third floor
1. Main room
2. Bathroom
3. Toilet
4. Multiuse space
5. Workshop
6. Guest room
7. Staircase

Fourth floor
1. Kitchen
2. Dining room
3. Staircase
4. Toilet
5. Living room
6. Terrace
7. Library

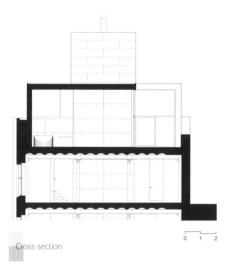

Cross section

0 1 2

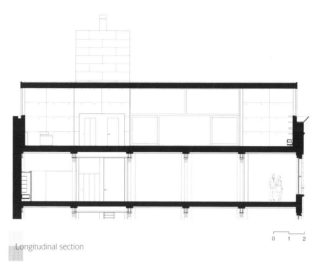

Longitudinal section

0 1 2

The project is located in the historic center of the city, very close to the bay, where many industrial buildings have been renovated. Because of their location and building type, they are ideal for mixed uses, as is the case here, where professional and residential activities have been combined.

The uppermost section of the building was covered with aluminum plates. Their reflection contrasts with the concrete of the rest of the building, bringing a luminous touch to an otherwise uniform gray line of roofs.

The library and the large living room are built around the terrace, which has splendid views of the city. The furnishings include pieces by the architect as well as classic twentieth century designs.

129

On the top floor, the greater part of the façade is glassed over, affording an abundant influx of natural light. To ensure adequate warmth, heaters have been installed all along the finishings.

The rooms feature warm materials: parquet flooring, painted or plastered walls, and wooden cabinets. The majority of the building's other walls are finished concrete surfaces which require strategically placed furniture to offset the hardness.

Thameside Dwelling

The client bought a 1,990 squarefoot shell on the fifth floor of an old warehouse beside the Thames. It has an irregular plan featuring a system of circular columns and beams, with a big window grid in revealed dark brick walls.

To organize the space and contrast with the existing irregularity, the project relies on a seventy-five-foot-long wall to separate the guest room, the utility room, the kitchen and the bathrooms from the large living room. This wall houses all the installations and is interrupted by a sharp break to let in light from the entranceway. The grid formed by the joints in the stone flooring reinforces the wall's role as the main geometric mass organizing the space. From the entranceway this wall creates a false perspective, directing the eye toward the views of the river. The armoire checks this false perspective and directs the eye toward the living room.

The end of the wall forms the head of the bed in the master bedroom, a room opened or closed at the occupants' discretion. The bedroom opens onto the large living room by way of a sliding door that is thirteen-feet high. An electric control system changes the glass divider, which separates the shower from the bedroom, from opaque to transparent. The bed is positioned to afford a view of the Tower Bridge through the windows.

The project was painted white and all the heating and lighting installations were concealed inside the walls to provide a neutral space that tastefully assimilates all the objects the client wishes to display.

Mark Guard Architects

Architects: Mark Guard Architects   **Photographers:** Allan Mower, John Bennet   **Location:** London, UK   **Completion date:** 1998   **Floor space:** 2,000 sq. ft.

Stainless steel rails in the stone
flooring allow the tables to be moved
around for varied uses.
The kitchen furniture can be used
as a serving cart or as an extension
of the dining room table.

The loft was painted white and all the installations
have been concealed so as to provide an open
space free of wiring or tubing that might interfere
with the perception of continuity. Locating all the
rooms on one side of the apartment created a
large, flexible, multiuse room.

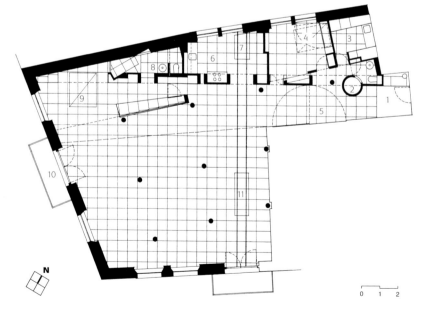

Plan
1. Entrance
2. Shower
3. Utility room
4. Folding bed
5. Swing door
6. Kitchen
7. Sliding metal table
8. Bath
9. Main room
10. Balcony
11. Sliding glass table

Loft in Chelsea

This project is set up in an old 1,200squarefoot clothing warehouse in Chelsea. This industrial neighborhood on the banks of the Hudson River is undergoing an astonishing transition like what happened in Soho: many of its factories are being converted into art galleries and apartments.

Given that its views of the city are not that interesting, the loft's design was governed by a desire to create a cohesive, calming group of interior spaces. The strategy used by the architect was to bring in as much light as possible to transmit absolute calm and repose.

The dwelling's frame is homogeneous and neutral to allow the furniture and other objects to stand out and define the space. The use of indirect light also mitigates any disturbance coming from the hubbub of the street.

The designer's intended depth of field is achieved through transparencies based on layers of translucent materials and sand-blasted matte glass, set off by a palette of light colors.

The loft has been conceived for a single occupant and the distribution is open so that each area's activities is free of any rigidly defined borders. This flexible layout is conducive to changing the furniture around frequently and creating new views.

The bathroom and toilet have no windows, so bright and translucent materials were brought in: mirrors, treated glasses and limestone to instill a distinctive, elegant touch to these intimate zones. Some pieces, like the bathroom dressing table or the aluminum plates on the dining room table, add to the spirit of the design by enhancing the light.

Kar-Hwa Ho

Architects: Kar-Hwa Ho   **Location:** New York, New York, US   **Photographer:** Björg Photography   **Completion date:** 1996   **Floor space:** 1,200 sq. ft.

Use of only a few materials brings a uniformity to the dwelling. The flooring is wood parquet and the walls are plastered. In the kitchen, stainless steel combines with the painted white wood of the cupboards.

The library is designed specifically for the project with prefabricated stainless steel strip mounts that are regularly spaced to create an ordered storage module. Some thin metal shelves are fixed into the back of the mounts.

1. Entrance
2. Living room
3. Kitchen
4. Toilet
5. Bathroom
6. Master bedroom

N

0   1   2

In spite of the lack of windows, the bathrooms are in no way claustrophobic or dark. The lighting was carefully designed and the materials strategically chosen.

O'Malley Residence

This loft in the small Pennsylvania town of Avoca was originally a warehouse. The building's perimeter was demolished, but the structure of columns, beams and walls that once made up the diaphanous, virtual mass remains standing.

The 1,500squarefoot dwelling was rehabilitated for the needs of a single occupant whose main requirement was conserving as much space as possible by incorporating important storage units. Thus, the layout was organized from the north wall, which houses the cabinets, and from the south front, where the kitchen and bathroom are located. Since only one person would be living here, transparent and translucent partitions have been installed in most cases. This makes for an interesting use of light, which flows abundantly through the openings in three of the four apartment walls. Free from the need for privacy, the rooms enjoy ethereal borders.

To make the most of the natural light which floods in from the south, the architects insured that light flows through the kitchen and bath. The former is dotted with translucent glass panels; the latter has a large horizontal cut doubling as a counter for dining room meals.

The flooring is an oak platform that includes marble bands that follow the pattern marked out by the round columns. Every passageway has a quality of light and sensation of space chosen to fit in with the architects' overall design concept.

Carpenter Grodzins Architects

Architects: Carpenter Grodzins Architects   **Photographers:** Chun y Lai Photography   **Location:** Avoca, Pennsylvania, US
Completion date: 1998   **Floor space:** 1,500 sq. ft.

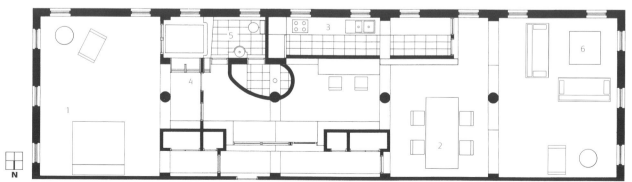

Floor plan
1. Bedroom
2. Dining room
3. Kitchen
4. Entrance
5. Bathroom
6. Multiuse space

0 1 2

N

Flanking the entrance, two cabinets of ash and glass suggest the idea of storehouse walls. This structure itself combines with the storage space to conceal the true function of the shelving.

The casual order suggested by the marble bands in the oak platform marks off the different areas, such as the dining room, living room or bedroom, without using vertical partitions that would interfere with the diaphanous, open space.

The bathroom combines wood, marble and mirror. It is the only totally closed-off space, although the translucent panels around it give it a certain visual permeability.

Four-level Loft

This project takes up the first floors of a building in the Gracia Quarter, a quintessential neighborhood near downtown Barcelona. The entire building was refurbished by the architect Joan Bach, who designed the first stories to accommodate an apartment for his own use, with an office included.

The uniqueness of the loft apartment lies in the creation of four differentiated levels that contain a space for each function without the use of walls. Except for the baths, the rooms are interconnected, at least partially.

The ground floor houses the entranceway, a small reception office and a bathroom. Use of a mechanically operated metal platform provides access to the bedroom and to the bathroom, which are located above the hall.

From the access floor, three steps descend to the double-height living room and to a handkerchief patio which, thanks to the low walls around it, brings abundant natural light into the apartment. The living room, with its increased height, has a small attic addition with a studio that affords exterior views.

The logic that led to such an ingenious layout also governs the décor criteria. The selection of furniture (some exclusively designed, others bought on the cheap), the exterior garden (Zen style) and the lighting create a relaxing and soothing atmosphere.

Construction details were carefully thought out to include fine finishes. The design solutions are oriented toward all the comforts of loft living. A good example of this diligence are the skylights, operated by an electric mechanism that opens their locks to increase overall ventilation.

Joan Bach

Architect: Joan Bach   **Photographer:** Jordi Miralles   **Location:** Barcelona, Spain   **Completion date:** 2000   **Floor space:** 1,340 sq. ft.

Photos on these pages show
the space from different angles.
The dwelling's ceiling height,
large windows and skylights
create wide spaces
and luminosity.

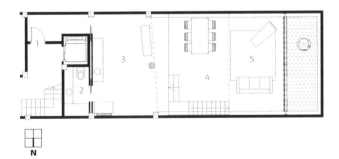

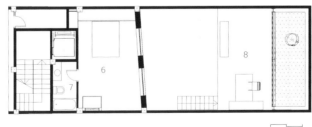

N

0 1 2

1. Entrance
2. Bathroom
3. Reception
4. Dining room
5. Living room
6. Bedroom
7. Bathroom
8. Studio

Silmu Residence

This dwelling is located on the ground floor of an old textile factory. The red brick building was constructed in 1928 in the historic center of Helsinki and was renovated and turned into apartments several years ago.

The ground floor originally served as the factory office and was later converted into a commercial space. In the eighties, all the beams were covered with a false ceiling and various floorings were added.

This project's objective was to uncover the factory's antique structure and convert it into an apartment with open space. All the vertical partitions were eliminated and the false ceilings removed. The steel beams were restored and some parts of the ceiling were painted with dyes. The brick, once cleaned, was rejoined using a mixture of beer and an agglutinating agent.

The wooden tie beams were reused as supports for the varnished pine floor that was installed on top of the original one. The architects improved the floor's acoustics by adding cellulose, which absorbs sound reverberations and cuts down on the noise made by walking. The architects left a space between the wooden floorboards and the walls in which to insert the heating pipes.

The L-shaped residence is organized so that the bathroom and kitchen occupy the smaller part of the apartment. A large living room and bedroom are located in the more spacious area that covers the building's entire dimensions.

The bathroom is housed in a new covered structure made of plywood that also contains, on one end, the oven and the kitchen cabinets. This new volume does not reach the ceiling in order to leave a space that can be used for storage.

Olli Sarlin & Marja Sopanen

Architects: Olli Sarlin & Marja Sopanen   Photographer: Arno de la Chapelle   Location: Helsinki, Finland   Completion date: 1997   Floor space: 910 sq. ft.

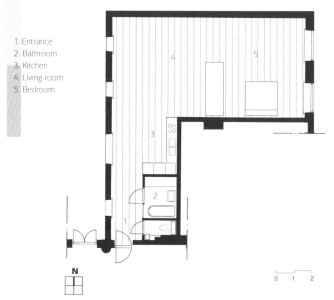

1. Entrance
2. Bathroom
3. Kitchen
4. Living room
5. Bedroom

N

0 1 2

The space housing the bathroom does not reach the ceiling height. This emphasizes the new mass and creates a small storage area above it.

All the elements that make up the residence are mobile and allow different divisions. The architects also used various recycled materials such as antique cabinets from a hospital, secondhand refrigerators and kitchen cabinetry that was originally designed for industrial use.

Renaud Residence

This 4,000-squarefoot loft in New York's Soho district is the home of a young banker. It is an ideal refuge from the professional stress and fatigue brought on by frequent transatlantic trips and an elegant and relaxed meeting point for his friends. The architectural remodeling job turned it into a quiet domestic space inside a thriving social center. The space reflects the character of the neighborhood where the peace and quiet of a residential zone merges with the bustle of the stores and galleries.

The loft's design explores the Modernist tradition of planes and masses, opaque and transparent, and the interaction of different materials. The project adopts the qualities of contemporary architecture yet respects what was previously there.

The dwelling is divided into two equal halves: the first satisfies public functions and is characterized by the way the plane surfaces, walls, and floors play off each other. The other half satisfies private needs by using a cherry wood partition as a boundary to hide the rooms. This zone is lit by a translucent window in the wall that lets light in but preserves privacy. The false ceiling is punctuated by skylights from the original structure.

The introduction of movement in the planes, like sliding doors or swing doors, brought out the relationship between the rooms and the perception of the whole. Light flows easily among the different areas.

The building process included elements created on the spot and others that were prefabricated, where the control and design demands were more rigorous. The overall aim was to relate the development of the construction with what came off the drawing board.

Cha & Innerhofer Architects

Architects: Cha & Innerhofer Architects   **Collaborators**: Kaz Morihata, Ali Turan Koluman, Christopher Moon   **Photographer**: Dao-Lou Zha   **Location**: New York, US   **Completion date**: 1998   **Floor space**: 4,000 sq. ft.

The architects designed the kitchen furnishings. The cabinets are cherry wood and the counters are stainless steel. The wall separating the kitchen from the hall is made up of a shelf and an etched glass window. These elements, penetrable to the gaze and of course to light rays, play a unique role in the perception of the spaces.

The walls and some of the pieces of furniture have geometric mortises. In some cases, these hooks are mere formal gestures, but in others, they are functional and can be used as shelves or small tables.

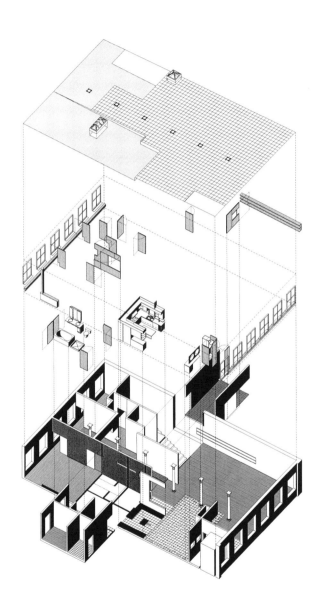

Axonometric perspective

The floor in the living room, hall and bedroom is made of maple wood. The floor in the television room, slightly raised, is walnut, and the floor in the kitchen and dining room are limestone.

1. Entrance
2. Dining room
3. Kitchen
4. TV room
5. Corridor
6. Master bedroom
7. Bathrooms

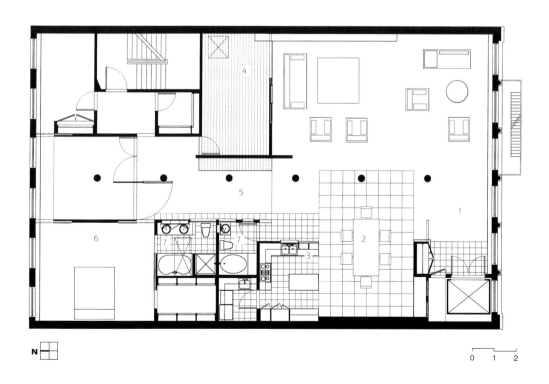

N

0   1   2

Goldsborough Loft

Glen Emrys and Pascal Madoc Jones, the two members of AEM, understood perfectly that the decision to convert a loft into a living space is not merely an aesthetic choice. Loft living means that the clients have a certain attitude toward life, and the architect must comprehend this alternative point of view.

One of the factors that comes into play is an attraction to open rooms and bare, unfurnished spaces. This commitment means, on one hand, that the architect must avoid dividing walls and must camouflage the storage spaces. On the other hand, the client must be able for a varirty of activities in a single space. In this London loft, the response to this choice led to excellent results. The chromatic treatment given to the few pieces of furniture present and the modeling of light through filters are not only faithful to the commitment to refrain from altering the existing structure, but they also manage to set free the potential lyricism of this type of space.

Except for the most intimate activities, which are isolated in the bathroom and bedroom, nearly all everyday activities take place in the large, main open space. The magic of this room stems from its emptiness, thus furnishings have been kept to a minimum.

All facilities—the pantry, kitchen, bath and sauna—are located in the inside perimeter of the loft, occupying the niches and recesses of the wall separating the living space from the neighbor and from the stairwell.

An acid-etched glass screen and a clothes closet are used to demarcate the two bedrooms.

AEM

Architects: AEM **Collaborator:** Peter Goldsborough **Photographer:** Alan Williams **Location:** London, UK **Completion date:** 1997 **Floor space:** 1,720 sq. ft.

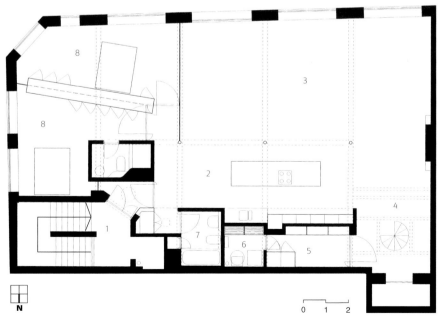

1. Entrance
2. Kitchen
3. Living room
4. Stairs
5. Storage
6. Sauna
7. Bathroom
8. Bedrooms

N

0 1 2

The architects' intention was to preserve the original open space without breaking it up into too many compartments. However, the acoustic and visual privacy of the bedrooms had to be assured.

Loft in Madrid

This loft is located on the ground floor of a detached block of apartments. Its front wall is twelve feet high and the wall at the opposite end of the large, well-lit gable-roofed bay is eighteen feet high.

Entry from the street is by way of an offset in the façade that incorporates an interior/exterior patio. This arrangement places the bedroom off the back hall, with ample lighting and ventilation coming through the intermediate space. Privacy is achieved by way of a metal screen between the street and dwelling, as well as the use of reflector glass in the windows.

The hall runs along the back, providing a glimpse of the wide open space of the bay, an enormous container that houses all the domestic functions. It is bathed in light from a roof-light that runs the length of the ridgepole, its lines broken only by the steel cables anchoring it to the walls.

The gray walls follow the configuration of the sloping ceiling like a single continuum interrupted only by the skylight. The meeting point of this plane and the floor along the whole length of the large living room is resolved through the use of a recessed baseboard that produces a continuous line of shadow to conceal the electrical installations.

The center of the floor contains the service areas, and three detatched walls establish the kitchen, the closet and the back storage space.

Lighting carefully differentiates the separate rooms, with a certain movie set style, both in the entrance and in the main bay.

Caveda Granero Romojaro Arquitectos

Architects: Caveda Granero Romojaro Arquitectos   **Collaborator:** Inés Higuera   **Photographer:** Maite Gallardo   **Location:** Madrid, Spain
Completion date: 1999   **Floor space:** 2,960 sq. ft.

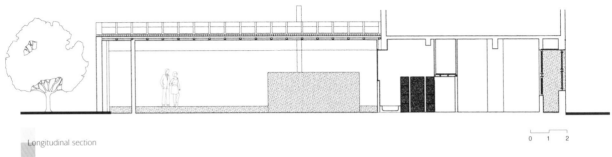

Longitudinal section

0 1 2

The gray tones of the walls, ceiling and flooring are splashed with bright colors emanating from some of the furniture and from the works of art.

Air-conditioning, a basic requirement for comfort in such a large, open space, was achieved through the installation of heating beneath the floor reinforced by a conventional ventilation system of revealed ducts.

The steel beams and the rails of the sliding doors are also exposed. The flooring in the entire bay is of polished concrete while the private areas are of industrial parquet.

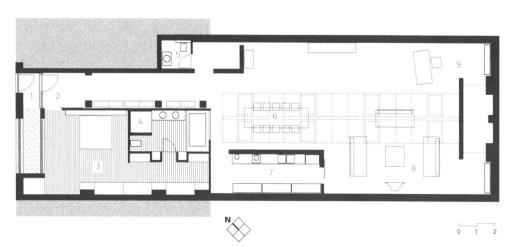

1. Interior courtyard
2. Entrance
3. Bedroom
4. Bath
5. Toilet
6. Dining room
7. Kitchen
8. Living room
9. Office

0 1 2

The kitchen and bathroom
walls are faced in stained
and varnished concrete mortar.
The same finish was used
on the building fronts.

179

Rosenberg Residence

The Rosenberg residence, a multiuse project in an early twentieth-century commercial building converted to living space during the 1980s, has made the most of a functional division. The decision to place the dwelling and studio on different levels has allowed the users to enjoy specific, distinct environments in the same apartment.

The project involves two 1,500 squarefoot floors. They are vertically connected, with the lower floor renovated as an office, studio and home for an art-loving resident. From the outset, this special relationship between the two units played a prominent role in the plan. The architects were able to develop a material language that paradoxically joins both parts and makes them independent.

On the upper floor, the dwelling contains a living room, a kitchen and two bedrooms. No partition breaks up the exterior wall, which lets in abundant light from the north. The lower level, with its restored, sandblasted concrete flooring covered in zinc casting, serves as an office and studio. Two mobile screens, one of plasterboard and the other of translucent glass, make it easy to rearrange the apartment. The two levels are connected by a staircase which seems to have come straight from a ship and which separates the work area and the living area on the upper floor.

A limited palette of materials (concrete, maple, stainless steel and laminated glass) has forged a space with simple yet elegant finishes. Some of the furniture, such as the cooking top in the kitchen and the bathroom, were designed by the architects themselves.

Belmont Freeman Architects

Architects: Belmont Freeman Architects   **Photographer:** Christopher Wesnofske   **Location:** New York, New York, US   **Completion date:** 1998   **Floor space:** 3,000 sq. ft.

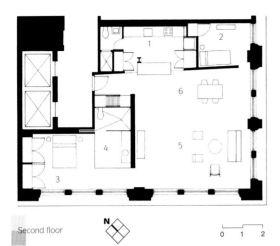

Second floor

N

0 1 2

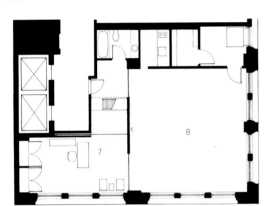

First floor

1. Kitchen
2. Bedroom
3. Bedroom
4. Bathroom
5. Living room
6. Dining room
7. Office
8. Studio

Hatchway-like stairs connect
the two levels and separate
the work area from
the private quarters
on the upper floor.

Views of the bathroom
and kitchen, both with
furnishings designed
exclusively for the project.

Calypso Hill

The promoter of Calypso Hill wanted to offer a new type of apartment, an original dwelling in harmony with postmodernist architecture. The loft's oval plan was entirely dominated by a 118-foot glass façade, which made many clients apprehensive. They were used to compartmentalized dwellings closed to the exterior. The challenge was to show prospective owners that it is possible to live in diaphanous spaces with generous views of the surroundings from every part of the house without relinquishing privacy.

The team of architects, Linda Arschoot and William Sweetlove, began work on the empty shell, made of eleven columns and two installational nuclei. The project's key idea was to create a large living room around which the other rooms were developed with, of course, spectacular views.

The aim was to inundate the apartment with changing light from the English Channel, often depicted in the paintings of Rembrandt and Rubens. It was also desirable to introduce views of a small chapel nearby and a typical Norman farmhouse situated on a dune.

A central passageway was laid out to separate the apartment into two parts. From its origin in the entranceway, the passageway provides stunning views. The left-hand side houses the master bedroom and bath; the right-hand side contains the storeroom and the laundry room. The passageway opens onto the non-partitioned spaces.

Heating is provided by a radiator system under the oak flooring. The architects custom-designed the storage units, the kitchen and the bedroom furniture.

Non Kitch Group

Architects: Non Kitch Group **Photographer:** Jan Verlinde **Location:** Oostduinkerke, Belgium **Completion date:** 2000 **Floor space:** 1,935 sq. ft.

Access to the upper-level terrace is by way of a spiral staircase at one end of the apartment. This element includes a load-bearing column, a series of thin rungs and a svelte handrail forming a stylized whole that avoids interrupting the splendid views seen through the large windows.

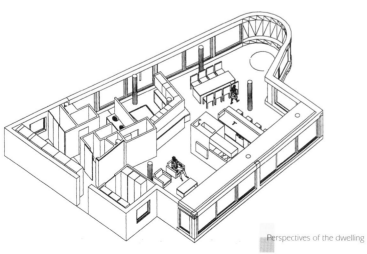

Perspectives of the dwelling

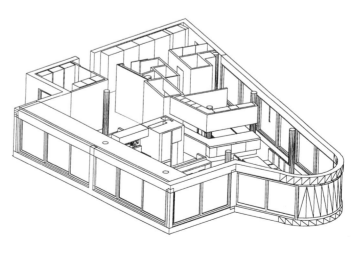

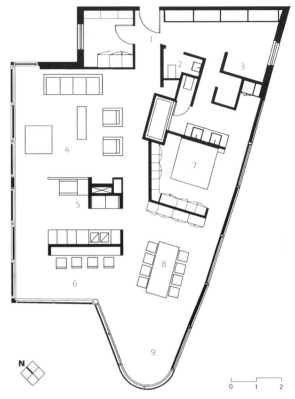

N

0 1 2

1. Entrance
2. Toilet
3. Bath
4. Living room
5. Kitchen
6. Bar
7. Bedroom
8. Dining room
9. Staircase

Except for the bathroom, all the rooms are open and interconnected. The kitchen is demarcated by two pieces of furniture, one high piece housing the appliances, and a low piece with storage units that doubles as a counter for light meals. The chairs were custom designed by the architects themselves.

Master bedroom privacy is achieved by way of curtains alone. Such borders are so ethereal and translucent that they blend into the views of the exterior.

Nile Street Loft

The apartment sits on the top floor and roof level of a four & five storey 107,500squarefoot nineteenthcentury warehouse. The brick building fronts onto four streets, filling an entire city block and forming a central courtyard.

The "shells" were left rough without any finishes. New capped-off services were located near the front door but the existing brickwork and floor slabs were left exposed.

The client's brief called for a one bedroom apartment with home office space and a multipurpose room capable of being closed off and used as a second bedroom.

The approach maximizes the sense of space by moving the unit's existing front door and creating a skylit double-height entrance hall which visually connects the two floor levels and contains all circulation areas. A skylight runs the full length of the top floor over this area spreading natural light deep into the plan. Several large sliding and pivoting fire-separation doors are carefully designed so that they practically disappear, ensuring a fluid relationship with the open plan living/dining/kitchen areas while retaining a good escape route in case of fire.

The existing external brick walls and concrete ceiling slab have been sandblasted and left as the original rough "shell" within which contrasting new elements in separate materials have been added to define the space.

The most important of the new elements is the African walnut wall boarding which forms a cohesive, predominant natural texture extending from the open kitchen to the entrance hall, up the double-height stair surround and finishing in the conservatory entrance.

McDowell & Benedetti

Architects: McDowell & Benedetti **Collaborators:** Brian Eckersley, Jeffrey Pickett **Photographer:** Nick Hufton/View **Location:** London, UK **Completion date:** 2000 **Floor space:** 2,000 sq. ft.

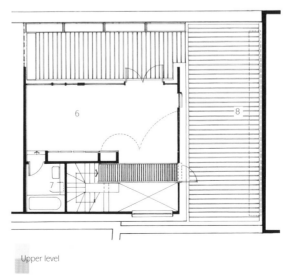

N

0 1 2

1. Entrance
2. Desk
3. Living room
4. Dining room
5. Kitchen
6. Bedroom
7. Bathroom
8. Terrace

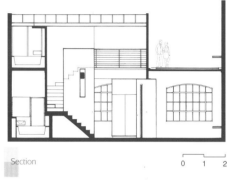

Section

0 1 2

The bedroom is in one of the
corners of the upper level.
The terrace was covered
with wood slabs and has
magnificent views of
the city skyline.

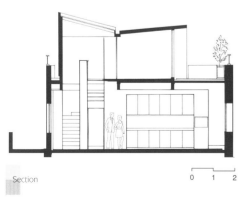

Section

0 1 2

Loft in Milan

The newest image of this loft, remodeled repeatedly through the years, merges past and present into a clear metropolitan identity. The development of the design offers a trip through the history of decorating fashion and allows the perception of spatial tensions which enrich the dwelling's spaces.

The commission entailed joining two autonomous units to create a single unified and flexible ambience. The result is a large space structured according to a relationship between its three main elements: a container for the living room, dining room and library; the simple trabeated framing system; and the rooms housing the private spaces such as the bathrooms, the dressing room and the bedroom.

One of the project's aims was to create two composite and structural systems that would diverge functionally but still complement each other to offer a warm, comfortable domestic space. Thus, a columnar system was created for the organization of the dwelling. This system also allows the positioning of small cubes that interrupt this structural rhythm.

The entrance was planned as a small area off the passageway between the kitchen and bath and leading to the dining room. At its widest point, beginning in front of a small table built around a column, it is less a transit area than an activity space. All the rooms with domestic functions radiate off this space. The corridor's perspective is then accentuated by the openings in the adjacent wall. The corridor contrasts with the luminosity and roominess of the large living room.

The architects designed some of the loft's furnishings with the aim of adding a touch of color to set off the white painted walls.

Laura Agnoletto & Marzio Rusconi Clerici

Architects: Laura Agnoletto & Marzio Rusconi Clerici   Photographer: Matteo Piazza   Location: Milan, Italy   Completion date: 1999   Floor space: 1,550 sq. ft.

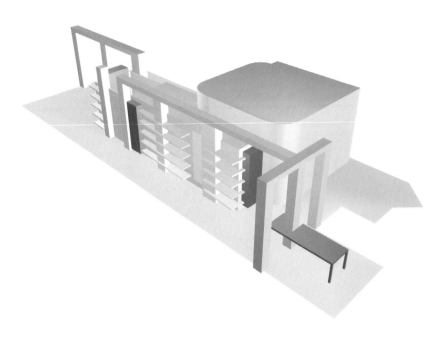

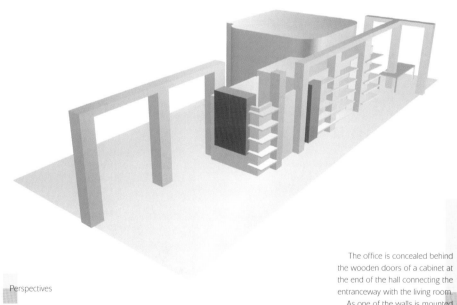

Perspectives

The office is concealed behind the wooden doors of a cabinet at the end of the hall connecting the entranceway with the living room. As one of the walls is mounted with shelves, the corridor also serves as a library.

205

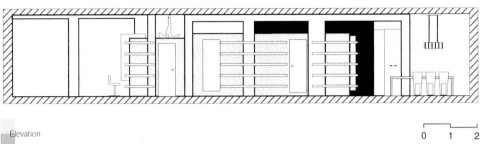

Elevation

0 1 2

1. Entrance
2. Kitchen
3. Bath
4. Dining room
5. Studio
6. Living room
7. Bedroom

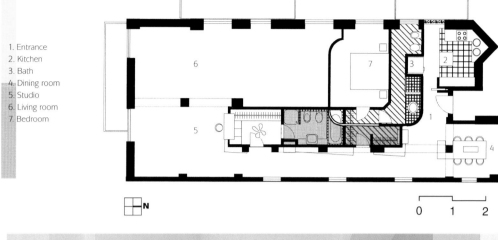

N

0   1   2

Wall Street Loft

In 1995, New York's City Hall encouraged contractors to convert empty office buildings in lower Manhattan into residential space. The city's revitalization plan offered tax incentives and flexible construction requirements. The real estate group Time Equities took advantage of the proposal and hired the architectural team Chroma AD to remodel a six-story building into thirteen lofts.

Wall Street, the New York financial area, is characterized by tall buildings and narrow streets. Often the only sunlight that reaches the façade of a building may be light reflected off another building. The dramatic shadows and piercing rays of natural light found in this area are the conceptual inspiration for this project. By creating luminous white boxes and punctuating them with black elements the architects hoped to reflect the feel of Wall Street.

Wall-to-wall windows and eleven-foot ceilings take advantage of all available daylight. Highly reflective epoxy-resin floors bounce light throughout the loft with a monolithic black kitchen and honed-black granite vanities that contrast with these "cloud-like" spaces.

Following the removal of commercial hung-ceilings, board formed concrete beams were exposed for the first time, many up to thirty-inches deep. The kitchen, bathrooms and open spaces were designed to harmonize with the existing ceiling beams and columns. The walk-in dressing room is equipped with industrial fittings and provides privacy and ample storage. The monumental bathroom is finished with imported porcelain tiles, custom-designed lighting and a six-foot granite counter.

Since the loft was designed as a live-in work space, all dwellings have various telephone lines, high speed cables and air-conditioning.

Chroma AD

Architects: Chroma AD **Photographer:** David M. Joseph **Location:** New York, New York, US **Completion date:** 1999 **Floor space:** 1,400-1,600 sq. ft.

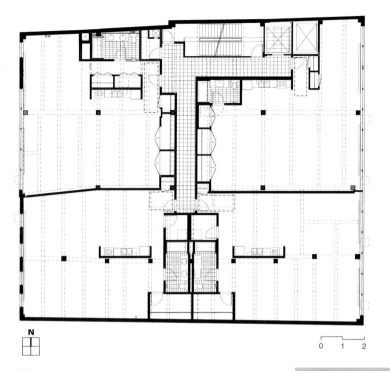

A general plan of one of the floors. Three kinds of lofts were created from a single design concept.

A view of the living room.

A view of the black kitchen and the dinning room.

N

0 1 2

The floor-to-ceiling windows bathe the dining room in light during the day.

The walk-in closets are spacious enough to serve as little rooms.

Abelow Connors Sherman Architects
T: 1 212 627 8866
F: 1 212 675 6199
www.acsarch.com
New York, New York, US

AEM
T: 44 20 7 7139191
F: 44 20 7 7139199
London, UK

Laura Agnoletto & Marzio Rusconi Clerici
T/F: 39 02 862623
Milan, Italy

Joan Bach
T: 34 93 5729501
Barcelona, Spain

Belmont Freeman Architects
T: 1 212 382 3311
F: 1 212 730 1229
New York, New York, US

Blockarchitecture: Zoe Smith & Graeme Wilson
T: 44 20 7729 9194
F: 44 20 7729 9193
mail@blockarchitecture.com
London, UK

Carpenter Grodzins Architects
T: 1 212 254 27 53
F: 1 212 254 2753
New York, New York, US

Caveda Granero Romojaro Architects
T: 34 91 7294796
F:. 34 91 294 819
Madrid, Spain

Cecconi Simone Inc.
T: 1 416 5885900
F: 1 416 5887424
Info@cecconisimone.com
Toronto, Canada

Cha & Innerhofer Architects
T: 1 212 477 6957
F:1 212 353 3286
www.cha-innerhofer.com
New York, New York, US

Child Graddon Lewis
T: 44 20 76362822
F: 44 20 76368377
cgl@lonw1.demon.co.uk
London, UK

Chroma AD: Raquel Sendra & Alexis Briski
T: 1 212 633 2700
F: 1 212 633 8220
Raquel.Sendra@worldnet.att.net
New York, New York, US

Jo Crepain Architects
T: 32 3 2136161
F: 32 3 2136162
mail@jocrepain.com
Antwerp, Belgium

Franc Fernández
T/F: 34 93 2000542
Barcelona, Spain

Mark Guard Architects
T: 44 20 73801199
F: 44 20 73875441
www.markguard.com
London, UK

Kar-Hwa Ho
T: 1 212 237 3450
F: 1 212 956 2526
KHo@KPF.com
New York, New York, US

Lichtblau & Wagner
T: 43 1 54518540
F: 43 1 54518544
Vienna, Austria

Helena Mateu Pomar
T: 34 93 3638060
Barcelona, Spain

McDowell & Benedetti
T: 44 20 7288810
F: 44 20 728844
London, UK

Moneo Brock Studio
T: 1 212 625 0308
F: 1 212 625 0309
New York, New York, US

Non Kitch Group:
Linda Arschoot & William Sweetlove
T/F: 32 58232723
nonkitchgroup@hotamail.com
Koksijde, Belgium

Resolution: 4 Architecture
T: 1 212 675 9266
F: 1 212 206 0944
New York, New York, US

Marco Savorelli
T/F: 30 02 8372048
Milan, Italy

Smith-Miller & Hawkinson Architects
T: 1 212 966 3875
F: 1 212 966 3877
New York, New York, US

Olli Sarlin & Marja Sopanen
T/F: 35 8 92784204
marja.sopanen@arrak.com
olli.sarlin@arrak.com
Helsinki, Finland

Tow Studios
T: 1 646 638 4760
F: 1 646 638 4761
New York, New York, US